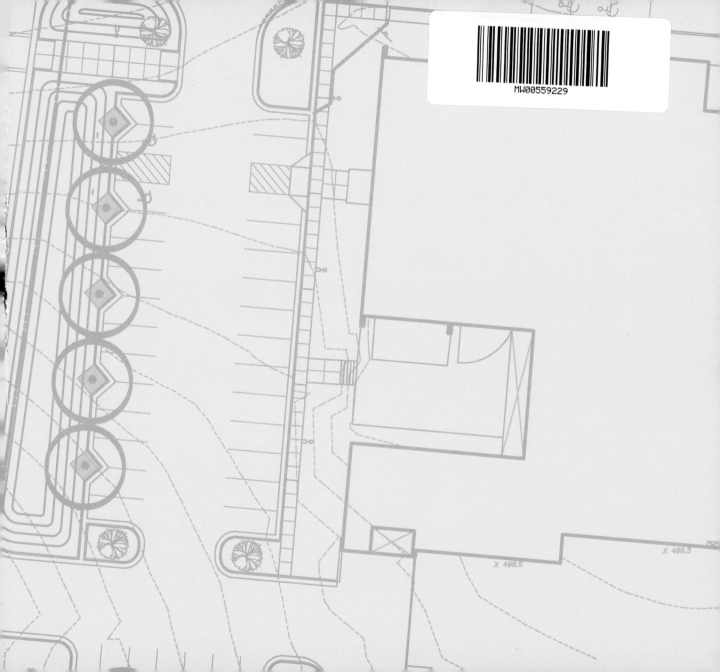

FRANK LLOYD WRIGHT'S
ROSENBAUM HOUSE

Frank Lloyd Wright - Rosenbaum House

Photograph by Patrick Hood; © City of Florence Museums

Frank Lloyd Wright's

Rosenbaum House

The Birth and Rebirth of an American Treasure

Barbara Kimberlin Broach
Donald E. Lambert, AIA
Milton Bagby

Originally published by Pomegranate Communications, Inc.

For more information about the Rosenbaum House, see www.wrightinalabama.com, www.florenceal.org
or call 256 760 6379.

Library of Congress Cataloging-in-Publication Data

Broach, Barbara Kimberlin.
    Frank Lloyd Wright's Rosenbaum House : the birth and rebirth of an American
treasure / Barbara Kimberlin Broach, Donald E. Lambert, Milton Bagby.
      p. cm.
    Includes bibliographical references.
    ISBN 978-0-7649-3763-7
      1. Rosenbaum House (Florence, Ala.) 2. Architecture, Domestic — Alabama — Florence.
3. Wright, Frank Lloyd, 1867–1959 — Criticism and interpretation. 4. Usonian houses — Alabama —
Florence. 5. Architecture, Domestic — Conservation and restoration — Alabama — Florence.
6. Florence (Ala.) — Buildings, structures, etc. I Lambert, Donald E. II. Bagby, Milton, 1947– III. Title.

    NA7238.F56B76 2006
    728'.373092—dc22   2006043267

Designed by Patrice Morris

Printed in Korea

CONTENTS

FOREWORD

In his book *The Master Builders,* Peter Blake wrote, "During the 1930's, Wright built four structures of a beauty unexcelled in America before or since." Three of those are Fallingwater, the Johnson Wax Administrative Building, and Taliesin West. The fourth is "really a structural prototype: the so-called Usonian house, a dwelling Wright developed in the late 1930's and executed, in several variations, during those years."[1]

The Rosenbaum House, an architectural treasure designed by Frank Lloyd Wright in 1939, was built for newlyweds Stanley and Mildred Rosenbaum in Florence, Alabama. It is one of the first half-dozen examples of Wright's Usonian concept.[2] The original 1,540-square-foot structure, with three bedrooms and two baths, was completed in the summer of 1940. When the Rosenbaums' household grew to include four sons, they called on Wright to enlarge the house. Wright's Usonian concept always anticipated a structure's expansion. The architect's 1948 addition, at 1,084 square feet, introduced a dorm room, a second, larger kitchen, and a guest bedroom.

Many authors have noted that living in a Wright-designed home could be the adventure of a lifetime.

This was true for the Rosenbaums, who owned the property for sixty years. Mildred Rosenbaum remained in the aging structure for years after her husband's death, occasionally opening it to the public as an informal museum. In 1999, when her health forced her to move, Mildred sold the house to the city of Florence with the understanding that it would be restored and turned into a working museum. The task would not be easy.

Frank Lloyd Wright's visionary designs often arrived ahead of the technology necessary to keep them functioning. The Rosenbaum House is no exception. The heating system, an in-slab hot-water piping network Wright called "gravity heat," failed. The only remedy would have been to jackhammer the entire floor in search of the problem. The house was warmed for decades by space heaters and through-wall air conditioners.

The elegant flat roof, built dead level, deflected in time, forming catch basins. The original roofing material, a cementitious slurry called Wearcote that was applied over hot tar, was no match for standing water: the first application cracked within months. Later repairs, which included a raised gravel stop and layers of heavy, water-repellent linen canvas, only aggravated the problem. The original cantilevered carport roof, almost twenty feet long and a signature feature of the house, developed an unnerving flexibility. Another cantilever extending from the 1948 addition had to be propped up with boards.

When the city of Florence purchased it in 1999, the house had reached a critical stage. Years of leaks had damaged the joists, ceilings, walls, and portions of the exterior trim. Termites had cored many of the walls. A city building inspector recommended that the Rosenbaum House be demolished.

The city completed the purchase anyway, developed a plan to save the house, and found funds to pay for it all. The acquisition and restoration of the Rosenbaum House might not have happened had it not been for the enthusiasm and substantial political will of the late Mayor Eddie Frost.

Dozens of volunteers, professionals, and tradesmen contributed to the work, but two citizens in particular teamed to see it through to conclusion. They are Barbara Kimberlin Broach, museum director for the city of Florence, and Donald E. Lambert, AIA, a principal in the Florence firm of Lambert Ezell Durham Architecture + Interior Design. Without their interest and hard work, the Rosenbaum House might have been lost. Their experiences form the core of this narrative.

This book is also a testament to Stanley and Mildred Rosenbaum, who faithfully cherished and protected the artistic intention of the house Wright designed for them.

We are grateful to the Frank Lloyd Wright Foundation at Taliesin West in Scottsdale, Arizona, for archival materials used in tracing the house's early history.

This book celebrates one of Wright's classic designs, rescued by Florence and its remarkable citizens, a treasure preserved not just for the people of that small town, but for the world.

—Milton Bagby

1. Peter Blake, *The Master Builders: Le Corbusier, Mies van der Rohe, Frank Lloyd Wright* (New York: W. W. Norton & Company, 1996), 379.

2. Alvin Rosenbaum presents a detailed portrait of the Rosenbaum family and what it was like to grow up in a Wright-designed house, as well as a treatise on Wright's Usonian and Broadacre City concepts as they played out in the context of Depression-era politics, the TVA, and Henry Ford's foray into the Tennessee Valley, in *Usonia: Frank Lloyd Wright's Design for America* (Washington, DC: Preservation Press, 1993).

Front view of the Rosenbaum House today, from Riverview Drive, shows long horizontal lines and few windows.

Photograph by Patrick Hood; © City of Florence Museums

Frank Lloyd Wright and the Usonian House

From 1936 until his death in 1959, Frank Lloyd Wright and his staff designed scores of private residences known as Usonian houses. Wright was sixty-nine when the first of these homes, the Jacobs House in Madison, Wisconsin, was built. *Usonia* was a term Wright claimed to have borrowed from Samuel Butler[1] to represent the United States and to symbolize his vision of an enlightened American society in which Jeffersonian ideals were combined with an advancing culture liberated from European influence. The Usonian houses he designed were meant to be a new form of affordable housing for the average American family. Open, airy, light-filled, with the lines blurred between inside and outside, the houses were to be emblematic of the personal freedom all Americans shared. Moreover, they were Wright's remedy for the traditional residential architecture he derided as "boxes within boxes."

While the Usonian concept was the result of years of Wright's experience—he had been, after all, an architect for half a century—the Usonians were also a product of external forces at work on Wright in the early 1930s.

The Depression brought about a decline in commissions for Wright. With few paying customers, he turned his mind to in-house projects that reflected the times and kept him in the public eye. The grandest of these was Broadacre City, Wright's melding of democratic ideals with early-twentieth-century urban design. The Broadacre model called for small city centers ringed with predominantly single-family and modest multifamily housing on farmlike acre-plus plots. All of it was connected by a network of modern roads that made commuting to work centers as convenient as possible. For the concept to work, Broadacre City would need housing that was affordable.

A mitered plate glass corner
demonstrates the Usonian principle
of blending inside with outside.

Photograph by Patrick Hood
© City of Florence Museums

Wright loved traditional building materials such as stone and wood—particularly red cypress—but he also championed new materials. Broadacre City led to experiments using modern and inexpensive building products such as concrete block and plywood. Structure was often the finished surface in Wright's program, resulting in a reduction in trim work and the substitution of unpainted for painted finishes. Nonetheless, savings did not always materialize.

Wright characteristically used these inexpensive materials in inventive and dramatic ways, making their installation, if not baffling to the average carpenter, certainly more labor intensive. Builders accustomed to covering up imprecision with plaster, paint, and trim now had to pay special attention to detail, which often meant increased labor costs. In many of Wright's buildings, wooden corners are mitered, another painstaking detail which requires more skill and time than conventional carpentry.

In reality, Wright may have had no intention of sacrificing his idea of beauty to save a dollar. "Stretch

Mitered cypress at the outside front corner of the study.
Photograph © Milton Bagby

yourself," he advised one client distraught at cost overruns. "Building this house is one of the best things you'll ever do. Stop for a while, if you must. I promise you'll thank me."[2]

It might be more accurate to say that Wright never fully intended to create affordable housing for the middle class so much as to make beautiful housing less expensive. By the end of the 1930s, new federal lending programs and an easing of the economic woes of the Depression combined to encourage home ownership. Wright, like other underemployed Depression-era architects, worked hard to make sure his housing ideas were ready if a recovery in the residential real estate market was at hand.

Wright was also influenced—whether he liked it or not, and mostly he did not—by the rise of modern architecture and the International Style. His inclusion in the 1932 exhibition of modern architecture staged by the Museum of Modern Art in New York was almost an afterthought, something between a patronizing acknowledgment of Wright's past glories and grudging admission that the old man had always pushed the boundaries of design and engineering.

His monumental ego undiminished by age, Wright welcomed inclusion in the show as his due and at the same time scoffed at his hosts and dismissed his fellow exhibitors. Wright downplayed its significance to him, but the MoMA exhibit may have been a watershed event that spurred him to the next level. If the fashion was modern architecture, then Wright would give the world something modern.

What followed was a remarkable string of designs, including Fallingwater at Bear Run, Pennsylvania, the Johnson's Wax Administration Building in Racine, Wisconsin, Auldbrass Plantation in Yemassee, South Carolina, the Honeycomb House in Palo Alto, California, and the early Usonian homes, which included the Rosenbaum House. It was a burst of creative productivity rarely equaled in any artist's life, let alone that of a man entering his eighth decade.

If Wright showed that he could design modern structures, the buildings were also affirmations of the organic principles he had extolled since his Prairie days: open space, light, human scale, simple materials. In Wright's skillful designs, scale and proportion play out in three dimensions to give these buildings a timeless, sculptural quality.

The living room of the Rosenbaum house is a superb example of the Usonian style, with a high ceiling, lots of glass, built-in shelves, and plenty of space.

Photograph by Patrick Hood; © City of Florence Museums

Wright answered the challenge of modernism, not with a defensive backward glance, but with the sure hand of a master more than prepared to move forward. Twenty years later, Wright would label the International Style with its characteristic glass skin as totalitarian. "The same old box," Wright snorted, "only now you really can look inside and see through the box and see that it is more of a box than ever." He also dubbed it "an evil crusade."[3]

Wright's Usonians might have been small projects with even smaller paydays, but they were a serious part of the public crusade Wright had made of his life's work. Residential commissions, which accounted for most of Wright's income, were also most likely to be seen by competitors, critics and—more importantly—future clients. Consequently, no Wright design arrived without relentless promotion from Wright himself.

Wright's urge to create a home for the average citizen was further prompted by the requests that poured in from youthful admirers, many of them college professors, young intellectuals, or forward-thinking professionals, who desired a Wright home but had no money for a mansion. The Rosenbaums,

well-educated sophisticates who lived and worked in Florence, Alabama, a sleepy college town on the banks of the Tennessee River, were typical of the clientele Wright tended to choose.

The first Usonians were, for the most part, small, flat-roofed houses organized with public functions in one wing and bedrooms in the other. At the junction of the wings was a service core typically containing the utilities, a kitchen—which Wright labeled the Work Space—and a bathroom. The core was contained in a mass of masonry that, in addition to having a fireplace, served as a base for the roof and an anchor for any cantilevered roof sections. The wings would correspondingly terminate in masonry. Wright kept the public areas of the Usonians at an impressive scale. Living rooms tended to be spacious, with higher ceilings, more glass, and room for amenities such as grand pianos, built-in benches, and bookshelves. He shrank noncommunal areas such as bedrooms and baths to their minimum functional size. Over the years, Wright placed the wings at various angles, depending on the organizing shape of the floor plan grid—at 90 degrees in the case of a right angle grid, at 120 degrees for an outside angle or 60 degrees for an inside angle, and occasionally at 45 degrees. In the earliest Usonian homes, however, the houses were typically laid out in a straight line or in wings set at 90 degrees.[4]

The first true Usonian was the Jacobs House of 1936, followed by the Rosenbaum, Pope, Goetsch-Winkler, and Euchtman Houses of 1939. There are other houses from the period—the Honeycomb House, so called for its arrangement on a hexagonal plan, the Bazzett House, another hexagonal plan, and the Rebuhn House—all of which use materials and have features similar to those of the Usonians. These include redwood or tidewater red cypress siding mounted horizontally in reverse board and batten, in-floor heating, a small central kitchen, and solid, uninsulated sandwich walls built of plywood or boards covered on both sides with cypress or redwood siding. Nonetheless, the defining characteristics of the pre–World War II Usonians include a modest single-story, flat-roofed design with a 90-degree or inline floor plan organized around two-by-four or four-by-four grids. As with so much of Wright's work in any period, it is hard to divorce one part from another. Many of his Usonian hallmarks turn up in projects not traditionally listed among the Usonians.

In time, Wright would expand the Usonian concept to include pitched roofs, curvilinear floor plans, and a greater use of both factory-made and hand-pressed concrete block. He tried to standardize components and dimensioning in later variations of the Usonians. Masonry-intensive editions, labeled by Wright as "Usonian Automatics," were homes reputedly so simple to construct that they almost built themselves. This was, of course, rarely the case.[5]

Wright habitually provided scant detail in the working drawings. He seemed to prefer that builders develop an instinctual feel for a structure and to believe that details would reveal themselves as the building went up. Where systems were simple and repetitive, as in the reverse board and batten he used on the interiors and exteriors of these houses, few details were necessary. Wright's oddly angled roof plans and dramatic cantilevers were another story.[6] On more than one occasion, the architect's apprentices went behind his back to suggest that carpenters install a flitch plate between roof joists or pour an extra load of concrete into the counterbalance of a cantilever.[7]

Several experimental subdivisions were developed around Wright's housing concepts, none more notably than at Usonia, New York, near Pleasantville in Westchester County.[8] Here, idealistic neighbors agreed to build their houses on circular lots, with the remaining land held in common. The homes were designed by Wright, his students, and outside architects who were more or less followers of his style. Usonian neighborhoods were also developed in Michigan, at Galesburg and at Parkwyn Village near Kalamazoo.

In 1953 Wright took a traveling exhibit of his life's work to New York, erecting the display on the site of what would become the Guggenheim Museum. The exhibit, titled "Sixty Years of Organic Architecture," was housed in a portable museum with a roofline canted dramatically in the fashion of Taliesin West, the site of Wright's Arizona home, fellowship, and school. Attached to the museum was a two-bedroom Usonian, a home for the heartland, put there for opinion makers on Park Avenue to see. In this same period, Wright worked tirelessly promoting Usonian home design through magazine articles, advertisements, and in a failed joint venture to build prefabricated Automatics.

Wright died in 1959. Many of his architectural and land-use theories have shown up in the real estate developed since his passing. Suburban shopping malls and office complexes surrounded by residential neighborhoods, parks, schools, and athletic fields, have an antecedent in Broadacre City. Indeed, Broadacre City, with its self-contained civic and business areas, was not so much a revision of small-town America as a prediction of present-day exurban developments no longer dependent upon the urban centers they surround.

While Wright's earliest Usonian projects had a sculptural purity that pushed the limits of popular taste, his later designs were imitated on a massive scale by developers who struggled to keep up with housing demand in the 1950s and 1960s. The Usonian, with its carport, cozy kitchen, and open floor plan, is in many ways the predecessor of the single-story ranch home. The imitations were not always successful. Developers were happy to cut corners and sacrifice design elements to stay on budget. Wright, unwilling to let the art of his concepts suffer, would characteristically dismiss rising costs and urge his clients to either bite the bullet or, in some cases, do the work themselves to save money; a number of clients did so.

More likely, the imitations failed because there was only one Frank Lloyd Wright. With the possible exception of Fay Jones in Arkansas and John Lautner in Los Angeles, few of Wright's students or followers have ever approached the mastery of the Old Man. Wright was at his best when he created the Usonians, working at a pace of productivity and level of artistry hard to imagine then or in any generation.

1. Frank Lloyd Wright, *The Living City* (New York: Horizon Press, 1958) and others. There is some question as to whether Wright or Butler originated the word "Usonia." Wright attributed it to Butler, yet had been using it himself for perhaps two decades as the name of his conceptual "United States of North America."

2. Roland Reisley and John Timpane, *Usonia, New York: Building a Community with Frank Lloyd Wright* (New York: Princeton Architectural Press, 2001), 141.

3. *House Beautiful* magazine, July 1953.

4. William Allin Storrer, *The Frank Lloyd Wright Companion* (Chicago: University of Chicago Press, 1993), 241 et seq.

5. Diane Maddex, *Frank Lloyd Wright's House Beautiful* (Washington, DC: Archetype Press, 2000), 128. Maddex is one of several authors who point out that Wright's projects almost always went over budget, even modest projects and even when the point seemed to be that of controlling costs. See also John Eifler and Kristin Visser, *Frank Lloyd Wright's Seth Peterson Cottage: Rescuing a Lost Masterwork* (Madison, Wisconsin: Prairie Oak Press, 1999), 10.

6. Reisley and Timpane, *Usonia, New York,* 140.

7. Donald W. Hoppen, *The Seven Ages of Frank Lloyd Wright: The Creative Process* (Santa Barbara, CA: Capra Press, 1993), 132. Hoppen describes how Wright's disciple Wesley Peters slyly suggested to owner Herbert Johnson that a trunk storage room be built beneath a dramatically cantilevered bedroom at Wingspread. Johnson agreed, Wright approved it, and Peters designed the trunk room with massive concrete walls to give extra weight to the counterbalance. Other stories in the Wright canon abound in which a jobsite fix was made, with the warning "Nobody tell the Old Man."

8. Reisley and Timpane, *Usonia, New York,* xiii.

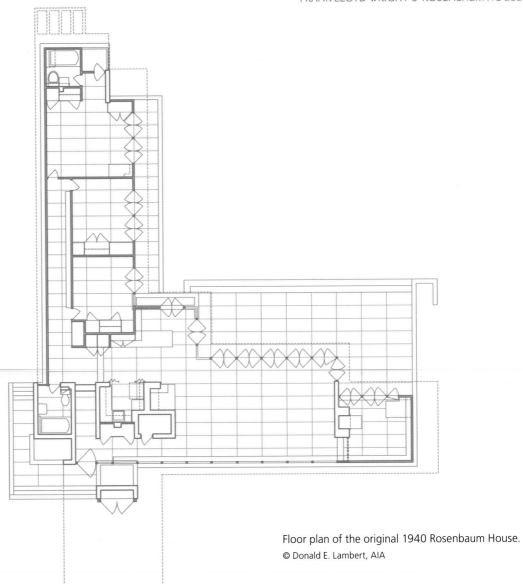

Floor plan of the original 1940 Rosenbaum House.
© Donald E. Lambert, AIA

Building the Rosenbaum House

IN April of 1939, Aaron Green, an architectural student living in Florence, Alabama, designed a house for his friends Stanley and Mildred Rosenbaum. When estimates for Green's design came in far over budget, he suggested to the Rosenbaums that they consider Frank Lloyd Wright. Green, who was in the midst of architectural studies at Cooper Union in New York, had seen and greatly admired Wright's 1936 house for Herbert Jacobs. He believed that the Rosenbaums would appreciate something similar.

"I suggested to the client, optimistically, that you be asked to design the house," Green wrote Wright, modestly adding that, "because your solution would be far superior to another's attempt in applying your ideas and philosophy, I would very much prefer your personal solution.

"The existing obstacle is a maximum amount of $7,500," Green noted a few paragraphs later, establishing the first budgetary line for the proposed house.[1]

Three months later, the young architect had an answer in the form of a two-sentence letter from Wright: "My dear Green: Will be glad to go through with a house for your clients. Perhaps you can follow through, with our assistance, in the execution."[2]

By mid-August, the Rosenbaums had Green send Wright a list of their needs: they wanted three bedrooms, two baths, a large kitchen with a service entrance and a pantry, a study, and a living room large enough to accommodate many books, a piano, an organ, and a radio-phonograph.[3]

Within days, Green received a letter from Eugene Masselink, Wright's secretary, thanking him for the information and advising him that Wright was already at work.[4] That note was followed shortly by another outlining Wright's fee schedule. Wright charged 10 percent of the estimated construction cost in installments of 3 percent for preliminaries, 5 percent for working drawings, and 2 percent for final supervision.[5]

Green answered that the Rosenbaums agreed to the fees, based upon a budget of $7,500. Green also asked Wright, ". . . Do you advise proceeding immediately with bidding when we receive your working drawings, or do you have in mind sending a representative at that point? What is the extent of your supervision?"[6]

Meanwhile, Wright's first sketches arrived in Florence. Stanley Rosenbaum promptly wrote Wright a check for $225 and enclosed it with a list of his observations about the drawings. There were problems with the use of an oil furnace for the gravity heat system. "We like oil heating because it is so clean, but unfortunately it is impracticable here. There is no servicing for oil heating equipment and the oil is not sold locally." Rosenbaum suggested that they switch to coal and, if possible, have a basement for the furnace and coal storage. "The kitchen seems rather small," he added near the end of the note.[7]

Wright responded that he would take care of the suggested changes. On the same day, Wright also wrote Green about the matter of project supervision, citing his reservations about the customary system of bidding and contracting. Wright implied that the special nature of his designs was better served by letting a Wright overseer parcel the work out on a piece rate. Such oversight came with a price.

"This throws a strain on us incommensurate with an architect's fee," Wright explained, "and we meet it by sending on an apprentice at the proper time to take charge, do shopping and hold the whole together — checking all layouts, etc.

"The owner is asked to lodge and feed him, pay his traveling expenses and pay the Fellowship $25.00 per week for his services so long as required —(it should not be in this case longer than ten weeks.)"[8]

In theory, the use of a Wright-trained apprentice was intended to speed construction, keep costs in check, and help local craftsmen learn the unusual Wright system of construction.

Green acknowledged Wright's letter. "Your terms are quite satisfactory to Mr. Rosenbaum and we shall try to make your man's stay here pleasant."[9] He also mentioned that he was bowing out of the process. With the pending arrival of an apprentice to supervise the project and with the Rosenbaums pleased with Wright's design, Green may have felt further participation on his part was unnecessary. He also may not have wanted to interfere with the work of the supervisor. In unsent first drafts of this letter, Green expressed his intention to someday apply for admission to Taliesin. Apparently Green reconsidered, and reference to training under Wright was dropped from the letter he finally sent.[10] In time, Green would study with Wright and become a valuable member of the Taliesin team, working for the firm's San Francisco office.[11]

As Green was writing his letter, Stanley Rosenbaum was telegramming Wright other news: "FIND HEATING OIL NOW POSSIBLE HERE. SORRY WE MISLED YOU."[12]

A month went by without word from Wright. After a gentle prod from Green—apparently not quite out of the process—Eugene Masselink sent copies of the specifications with a promise that the drawings were on the way. In the meantime, Masselink wrote, "Mr. Wright suggests you can do a little preliminary skirmishing until our man can get down to you."[13] The building instructions were only five pages of double- spaced type in length, typical of Wright's preference to let the building reveal itself during construction—so long as the revelation was approved by Wright, of course.

Like other early Usonians, the Rosenbaum house had a nominally flat roof, but the specifications made provision for runoff. "The framing of the roof is to be made of three 2x4s, one upon the other. Braced up to the required pitch of 1/8 inch to the foot—the 2x4s are to be toe-nailed together to hold this pitch."[14]

The specs also called for a roofing compound under the brand name Wearcote. Green, who had started checking on the availability of the materials specified, informed Wright's office that Wearcote was not locally available. He also noted that the three local suppliers favored by the Rosenbaums had all provided rough estimates that were too close to make any competitive difference.[15] Wright was still working on the final drawings in mid-November. By December, any chance to start the house during fall's mild weather was past.

On December 5, Wright wrote letters to both Green and the Rosenbaums introducing them to Burt Goodrich, the Taliesin apprentice who would help them build the house. A twenty-eight-year-old New York native with a degree in architecture from the University of New Hampshire, Goodrich had already studied with Wright for five years. Goodrich was in Wright's estimation, "cautious, and slow, but reliable and I think competent to get what both you and I want.

"I hope you will like Burt," Wright concluded, "He has the answers you need."[16]

Working drawings must have accompanied Goodrich, for Stanley Rosenbaum alerted Wright of his arrival in Florence and enclosed a check for $375, the next amount due.[17]

Goodrich was quick to size up his new associates. On his first day in Florence, he wrote that Green was "a young fellow (younger than myself by perhaps a couple of years) who is in the process of building his first house, so I won't expect too much in the way of actual building experience from him."

Of the Rosenbaums, Goodrich summed them up as "a young married couple . . . anxiously awaiting, not a baby, but a home." He described Stanley as "sort of an assistant to his dad who is the theater magnate in these towns—called the Tri-Cities. It is he from whom the money is to flow." Goodrich suspected that Stanley's father, Louis, would be "keen on how and where the money goes—his pride no doubt. So I intend to have him in on such matters to make things run along smoothly."

Goodrich also noted about the senior Rosenbaum, "Being a monopolist himself, he favors dealing with the other ones in town so it looks like dictated prices on material and union labor will have to be paid." Goodrich added that when he warned them that union labor and material bought at uncompetitive prices would drive up costs, they told him they had to follow that path in order to stay in the good graces of their neighbors.

"Mr. Wright, this is the low down on the situation as far as I have been able to determine to date."[18]

Goodrich had driven from Spring Green, Wisconsin, to Florence in a Bantam automobile, one of several owned by Wright. On learning that Burt had reached Alabama, Eugene Masselink inquired about the car in the opening sentence of his letter.[19] Masselink wrote from Arizona, where Wright and the Taliesin crew had just arrived to take up winter quarters. The Bantam, a sporty subcompact based upon the English Austin, was manufactured only between 1938 and the beginning of World War II. The car driven by Goodrich couldn't have been much more than a year old, but it was already a constant headache.

Only three days later, Masselink was urging Goodrich to finish as quickly as possible. "Mr. Wright does not wish to have you stay in Florence any longer than necessary to get prices, costs and organize the building of the Rosenbaum House." Wright had another reason for moving Goodrich along. He wanted Goodrich to go to Milwaukee and take delivery of a new Lincoln Zephyr—a Continental Club Cabriolet—and drive it out to Taliesin West. Along the way he was to stop in Des Moines and pick up another Wright toy, the Dinky Diner, a diminutive chuck wagon Wright used to feed his crew on long cross-country trips. It had been abandoned at a student's house when it lost a tire. Goodrich was to tow the diner behind the Zephyr over wintry two-lane roads from Des Moines to Phoenix.

The assignment must have dismayed Goodrich, who had barely arrived in Alabama to begin what promised to be a remarkable building project. He quickly protested. "Mr. Wright, I don't like to see such apparently ideal clients disappointed by getting the feeling that they have been left up in the air, when so willing to do all they can. Believe me, Mr. Wright, I want to be back with the Fellowship as soon as possible, for living as I am has no charm to me, but I feel I also need the experience. Wouldn't it be possible for Bob to bring the Zephyr down if you need it right away?"[20]

"You need not worry about the Zephyr," Wright instructed Goodrich shortly after Christmas. "Get away from the job when you are not absolutely necessary."[21]

The Zephyr was not the only problem facing Goodrich. He had been in Florence for a month and made little progress. On January 4, he wrote Wright that the bids had opened at "the ridiculous amount of $10,500." He had pushed the numbers around and gotten the price down to $9,000, which he said Stanley Rosenbaum would approve. He asked Wright for various changes, such as substituting electric heat for the oil-fired boiler—Stanley Rosenbaum had become sold on the idea that electricity would be more economical than heating oil—and less expensive single-strength glass instead of plate for the decorative lantern sashes. Goodrich complained that the weather had turned against him. There were two inches of snow on the ground. Freezing temperatures were a problem when there was concrete to pour or brick to be laid.

To make matters worse, his girlfriend had left him for another Taliesin student. In a handwritten postscript, he lamented, "Mr. Wright, my heart dropped out of me on hearing that Lucy intended and did leave the Fellowship. I loved her and hoped and believed that she would make good, but evidently she not only wouldn't (or couldn't) and even turned to another in my absence. I thought she would understand."[22]

Wright sympathized with the young man's heartbreak, even if his earthy words of comfort were a little left-handed. The girl, Wright noted, "is no loss, believe me. We took her in here for your sake but she is really a dumb Dora where anything you are vitally interested in (above the upper region of your pantaloons) is concerned. She was arm in arm with Gordon (who has dropped her) all the way out to camp, etc. etc. Here's hoping for a speedy recovery from her. What she meant to you some girl will really be someday. What's the hurry?"[23]

Goodrich spent the better part of January taking bids and helping the Rosenbaums with contracts for materials. There were three days near the end of the month when Goodrich could get a crew to work prepping the site, but before footings could be poured, the temperature dropped again.[24] By the time the footings were in and retaining walls under way, it was mid-February. Goodrich had been in Alabama for the projected ten weeks and Stanley Rosenbaum had already spent $250, plus room and board on account. Goodrich proposed to Wright that Rosenbaum be allowed to reduce the fee from $25 per week to $15 per week. Wright customarily split the fee in half with his apprentices, but Rosenbaum wanted Wright to take the reduction, not Goodrich. The young man mentioned this to Wright, but offered to split the reduction. Plainly, Goodrich had become invested in the project and was reluctant to turn over the house to Green or local contractors. "Now that the actual construction has begun on the house it is much more interesting. I hope to be allowed to continue my work here."[25]

Wright came quickly to the point. "Rosenbaum is supposed by the terms of his agreement to pay the expenses of your trip there and back, to shelter and feed you only while you are necessary to the work there. $25.00 per week he should pay to the Fellowship— that's me in such case—half to be retained by you— half sent to us. Has Rosenbaum done this?

"If so, I am willing to let up on him from February 15th forward, but we cannot afford to deduct a membership for more than eight or ten weeks to get one little house built, Burt."[26]

Wright could be imperious and blunt. His students lived for his praise and agonized under his criticism.[27] The young apprentice, evidently stung by the master's tone, confided in the client. Rosenbaum quickly wrote Wright in support of Goodrich. "My wife and I both like Burt very much and we would certainly dislike losing him with the work scarcely begun. We would greatly appreciate it if you could see your way clear to let him stay here until he can see the thing through. On the few

A warm, clear day—one of too few—in the spring of 1940 let workers make progress on the slab. Looking east from the patio. Standing brickwork is the carport closet.

Photograph courtesy The Frank Lloyd Wright Foundation, Taliesin West, Scottsdale, AZ

days on which work was possible, progress was rapid, and I think a few weeks of reasonably good weather would suffice."[28]

Goodrich defended himself, writing that he had only tried to do what Wright had instructed him. As for Stanley Rosenbaum paying the $25 weekly fee, "He has done that. I have retained that as you told me to. I have spent some of it on a transit, tape and some drafting incidentals which I consider Fellowship equipment."

Even so, Goodrich said he was preparing to leave

Alabama, provided they could take care of problems with the company car. "Before starting out I shall have to buy a new tire, and have new piston rings put in the Bantam. It burned 16 quarts of oil in the 800 miles from Taliesin to Florence; 2000 miles [from Florence to Arizona] would mean using 40 quarts.

"No doubt, Mr. Wright, this little house has assumed over-important proportions in my mind, but I cannot help feeling disappointed in that this greatly desired experience of building one is to be once again put off

FRANK LLOYD WRIGHT'S ROSENBAUM HOUSE

Late spring, 1940. Low roofs are coming up. Traditional houses across the street demonstrate the contrast Wright's design will provide.

Photograph courtesy The Frank Lloyd Wright Foundation, Taliesin West, Scottsdale, AZ

into the future. I am definitely preparing to leave as soon as things can be arranged for the house to go forward without me."[29]

Wright, apparently judging from the tone of Goodrich's letter that his apprentice was becoming demoralized, telegrammed a response. "TELL ROSENBAUM WILLING YOU SHOULD STAY ANOTHER MONTH TO PUSH THINGS ALONG."[30]

A month wasn't enough. Thirty days later, on March 27, Wright, having heard little news from Alabama, wrote Goodrich for cost figures and construction photographs.[31] Goodrich sheepishly replied, "Really,

Mr. Wright, it has been my continual disappointment in the quantity of work I have been able to get done that has made me reluctant to write to you." There had been four working days in January, two in February, nineteen in March; "Many of thes [sic] were not full days, either."

Goodrich reported that he had poured about half of the slab and completed several of the brickwork piers. He ended the letter with the unwelcome news that the state of Alabama wanted Wright to pay $30 for a license to practice architecture in Alabama and that Goodrich had to pay $55 for a superintendent's

The two wings of the 1940 house take shape.

Photograph courtesy The Frank Lloyd Wright Foundation, Taliesin West, Scottsdale, AZ

license.[32] This made no sense to Wright, who had never paid more than $5 for a license in any other state. He would do battle with the authorities over the matter of licensure for the remainder of the project.

The weather relented and Goodrich was at last able to make progress. By the end of the first week of April, he had started framing walls and roofs for the study and the bedroom wing. The living room fireplace and nearby bathroom walls were up about three feet. By the second week, Goodrich reported that all the roofs would be framed within two days. As instructed, he furnished Wright with photos and cost estimates. The

costs were already soaring, but Goodrich blamed this on modifications and the passive stance the Rosenbaums insisted on taking with local suppliers. Goodrich also wanted to know when he could expect information on the furniture Wright was designing for the house.

The Rosenbaum House was beginning to take shape. By the end of April, Goodrich was applying the roofing, wiring was being installed, and the cypress walls were being assembled. Goodrich was involved in details. Finding suitable hardware was a problem. Wright had specified that the doors have piano hinges, which were unavailable. "Piano hinges are unheard of here. Any suggestions? The very few people that have apparently made the effort to see and hear a piano failed to observe that it had hinges."[33]

Goodrich had been on the job now for twenty weeks. The work, which had seemed unending, was coming to a conclusion. By mid-May, Goodrich would write that he expected to finish soon. Of the long delays, he cited the weather, a scarcity of certain materials and the lack of tradesmen trained in building a Wright design. But he reserved his harshest criticism for himself. "The house has dragged terribly due to

Doors were custom built on-site. The brass piano hinges Wright specified for them proved hard to obtain.
Photograph © Milton Bagby

several reasons, no doubt the greatest being my lack of experience in organizing the work and the handling of the men," he wrote.

"I hope to be coming back to Taliesin soon as I'm getting awfully tired of this place and I'm homesick, missing the life and spirit that is only there."[34]

Wright's flinty response was to again urge Goodrich to send in the Fellowship's half of the fee.[35] Three weeks later, Masselink broached the subject again. "Why don't you send in an accounting on the money Mr. Rosenbaum has given you. Blaine [another Taliesin apprentice sent out on a project] has been sending in the $12.50 due the Taliesin office regularly. You should do the same. Half each week was to go to you and half was to come here, you know."[36]

Goodrich promptly sent in funds to Taliesin. "I'm enclosing some Fellowship money, proving that it hasn't been squandered. I have had to spend quite a bit on transit, architect's license and for repairs on the Bantam. No one is getting rich on this venture unless it is I, in experience."[37]

As the house neared completion, an unforeseen problem arose. Portions of the long walls of cypress board and batten were buckling outward at the top.

Walls and roof are up by summer, but the brick parapet and chimney remain unfinished. Parked out front is the infamous Bantam, one of a fleet Wright kept.

Photograph courtesy The Frank Lloyd Wright Foundation, Taliesin West, Scottsdale, AZ

Worse, the living room roof seemed ready to fail. Goodrich pressed Wright for a solution. A sketch sent by Wright did not solve the problems. "IMPOSSIBLE TO HOLD UP LIVING ROOM ROOF WITHOUT I BEAMS. TRIED FLICH [sic] PLATES AND HANGING BY THE RODS."[38] Flat steel plates fastened to a board or sandwiched between two boards to act as a stiffener and give additional strength, flitch plates are useful for increasing the linear strength of wooden beams with longer than standard spans. Wood has a natural tendency to deflect—to bend or bow in the direction of gravity under a load—and flitch plates can help

prevent this problem. Steel I-beams take the process a step farther, in that the shape of an I-beam prevents it from bending side to side, as well as up and down.

Wright quickly agreed to use I-beams. "RIDICULOUS OVERSIGHT IN THE PLAN SECTIONS. ONLY LIGHT TWELVE STEEL BEAM WILL CARRY ROOF. TAKE OFF TRIM BOARD AND PUT STEEL ALONGSIDE WOOD BEAM NOW PLACED. COVER WITH CYPRESS TRIM."[39]

No sooner were the structural problems of the house solved than, as if on cue, the Bantam automobile broke down. Goodrich begged Wright for the money to fix the crankshaft and replace the main bearings. "This car is certainly proving far from economical," he dryly observed.[40] He would need the car very soon, he wrote, for his return to Taliesin in Spring Green, Wisconsin, the site of the Fellowship during the summer months.

One month later, Goodrich was still in Alabama. "It has rained for the past two weeks," he complained. "It blew so hard the water penetrated the brick walls wetting the plywood ceiling in several places. . . . The painfull [sic] result was a state of panic for the clients and a big headache for me."[41] In addition to finding a remedy for the leaks, he was also waiting on a shipment of cypress plywood for the doors and busying himself with incidental furniture designs.

Summer, 1940. Rear of house, all but finished.
Photograph courtesy The Frank Lloyd Wright Foundation, Taliesin West, Scottsdale, AZ

By now, the building had become a sensation in the little town of Florence. In a letter to a friend, Stanley Rosenbaum reported that the house was getting as many as one hundred visitors a day, and up to five hundred on weekends. One visitor stared at it for a long time, then asked Stanley, "What is it?" Despite widespread curiosity, he related that perhaps no more than a dozen locals had expressed unreserved admiration for the bold little house. The letter closed with Stanley hoping his new home would be ready by August 1.[42]

In late July, Wright had Masselink contact Rosenbaum. He wanted to know how things were going. Rosenbaum wrote an extended response that summed up much of the history of the building process. It is a litany of problems encountered and solved, but always with attendant delay and at additional expense, which he attributed to Goodrich.

"The only criticism which I have to make of him is that, if there is any obvious omission or oversight in the plans or specifications, he goes ahead and follows them anyway and then afterwards has to do it all over again, at my expense." He softened the criticism by admitting that the house was experimental in many ways and

Front of the Rosenbaum House today from Riverview Drive. During construction, one visitor asked Stanley Rosenbaum, "What is it?"

Photograph by Patrick Hood
© City of Florence Museums

that Burt had worked very hard and continuously. The letter ends with Rosenbaum's pledge that "our enthusiasm for the house and for your plans has not abated one whit."[43]

On August 11, Goodrich was once again apologizing to Wright for not keeping him informed: ". . . So much of the time I have spent down here has been in a depression that I could not muster up enough enthusiasm to write."[44] When he promised this time that he would be coming back to Taliesin soon, he was right. On August 23, 1940, Stanley Rosenbaum wrote to inform Wright that he and Mildred had occupied the

house and that Burt would be leaving for Taliesin in a day or two. In the end, Burt Goodrich's sojourn in Florence would come to thirty-six weeks. The Bantam, still in need of work, made it as far as Terre Haute, Indiana, before dying.

Aaron Green, the young architecture student and friend of the Rosenbaums who had first introduced them to Wright, chose this time to visit the master at Spring Green. He would be admitted to Taliesin that fall as a new apprentice. Near the end of the Rosenbaum project, he had suggested to Stanley and Mildred that they call the house "Cypressonia," after its beautiful

Cypress reverse board and batten, a signature element of early Usonians, covers the front facade. Except for shallow windows at the roofline and a clerestory, the building is closed off from the street for privacy.

Original Pella folding door closed off the tiny kitchen in the 1940 house.

Photographs © Milton Bagby

siding. The Rosenbaums gamely followed Aaron's suggestion for a short while, but there is no evidence that the name stuck.

In September, the Museum of Modern Art sent G. E. Kidder Smith to Florence to take photographs of the new house for an exhibition they were planning. Smith's photos show the house in pristine form, unhidden by shrubs or trees. An interior picture illustrates Wright's Usonian furniture placed about the living room, a grand piano against one wall, and long bookshelves leading the eye toward Stanley's cozy study.

By now, a final accounting of costs could be assembled. The result, while no surprise, was still a shock. The completed project, originally estimated at $7,500, now totaled $14,347, almost double.

Wright continued to argue with the state of Alabama over the amount of any fee he should pay to be licensed, politely stalling until the job was finished before he sent them a note in effect telling them off: ". . . Don't you think thirty dollars is fee enough for building a $10,000.00 house in your state? If I ever build another (and I guess I won't) I might want to be an Alabama architect. You wouldn't pay $55 for the privilege of losing time and money on a small house, yourself, if someone asked you to build one in Wisconsin, would you?"[45]

The exhibition at the Museum of Modern Art gave the house a wave of international publicity. If the Jacobs House was the first of the true Usonians, the Rosenbaum House was its logical extension. Wright's designs from 1939 alone would have been enough to earn him a lasting reputation. The projects, mostly completed in 1940, include:

House for Andrew F. H. Armstrong, Ogden Dunes, IN

House for Sidney Bazett, Hillsborough, CA

House for Joseph Euchtman, Baltimore, MD

House for Lloyd Lewis, Libertyville, IL

House for Rose and Gertrude Pauson, Phoenix, AZ

House for John C. Pew, Madison, WI

House for Loren Pope, Falls Church, VA

House for Stanley Rosenbaum, Florence, AL

House for Bernard Schwartz, Two Rivers, WI

Auldbrass House and Plantation buildings
for Leigh Stevens, Yemassee, SC

House for George Sturges, Brentwood Heights, Los Angeles, CA

House for Kathrine Winckler and Alma Goetsch, Okemos, MI [46]

There was still a surprise waiting for Stanley Rosenbaum. In March 1941, Wright sent Stanley a polite note asking that the Rosenbaums settle their account with him for architect's fees, over and above the original fees, to cover the cost overruns. Wright cited a finished cost of $12,777.84, on which he had not been paid an additional $677.78 in fees.

"I wonder if you could clean this up with us now," he asked.[47]

Stanley responded with a measured, lengthy recounting of the cost overruns, the experimentation

Dining area, 1940 house. A wraparound table just steps from a tiny kitchen put the cook of the house more in touch with family and guests than traditional home designs.

Photograph © Milton Bagby

End of the bedroom wing, with a tiny one-person balcony just outside the master bedroom.
Photograph © Milton Bagby

involved, and Burt's lack of experience. The most troubling revelation in Stanley's letter was news that the Wearcote roofing surface had cracked all over and was failing, "so that when it rains now, we get leaks all over the house for several days after," Rosenbaum wrote. "Besides the embarrassment and inconvenience, this has also ruined more of the plywood ceiling. I am now going to have the roof fixed at considerable expense." Rosenbaum also complained that the decision to use an electric boiler instead of heating oil was costing a fortune, with monthly electric bills of $50 and $60—so high that it made sense to replace the system before the coming winter.

"All this has not prevented us from loving the house. We do, Mr. Wright, and we appreciate it; but we do also feel that, in view of everything that has happened, the books should be balanced as they stand."[48]

Wright relented, arguing only two points.

"My dear Mr. Rosenbaum: Of course you are about right. Concerning the roof however, the Wearcote is intended only for insulation not to keep out water. The roof must be tight before it goes on. The electric heat Burt tells me was installed upon the advice of a local engineer with your own approval."[49]

Wright's roofing specifications had called for the installation of four plies of tar paper. For an unknown reason, this was reduced to three plies during construction. Tar paper is water repellent but hardly waterproof, especially when laid flat and subjected to standing water. Wide-roll rubber and plastic roofing products were not yet perfected when the house was designed. The delicate spider work of two-by-four roof joists may not have been strong enough to carry the load of a more proven roofing system such as tar and gravel. Whatever its properties as insulation, it is clear that the Wearcote was partially intended to seal the

Bedroom wall reveals the richness of the grain in the wide cypress paneling.
Photograph © Milton Bagby

roof. It may have been an inferior product or it may have been improperly applied, but the result is that the roof leaked from the first.[50]

Burt Goodrich returned to Taliesin and remained an associate until 1946. He went on to have a long career as an architect and planner. Despite his youthful inexperience going into the Rosenbaum project, he is still responsible for building a great building, one of Wright's finest. He persevered in the face of real difficulties—weather, scarce materials, untrained craftsmen, even a broken romance and an unreliable car. He worked in the tradition of all Wright apprentices: learning by doing, an experimental process which by definition entails making mistakes and learning from them. Wright put him out there not only to learn how to build, but to teach him to let a building speak to him. In the end, Goodrich displayed great fidelity to everything Wright intended, seeing each detail to its conclusion and ignoring repeated chances to flee a difficult job. That some of the opportunities to leave the Rosenbaum project early came from Wright himself might suggest that the master was testing the apprentice.

The Rosenbaums were aware of the unique nature of their home. They were quite proud of it. The house not only broke with typical traditional residential styles, it was fluid and poetic. There was nothing like it in the South, and but a handful like it in the world. Wright was an artist and the Rosenbaums lived in a work of art.

If the Rosenbaums felt any animosity toward Wright about the cost of the house or some of its design flaws, it was overweighed by the pride they took in owning a genuine Wright design. And if they held any reservations about working with Wright again, those were forgotten in short order. Stanley and Mildred, with a quickly growing family, would soon call on Wright to help them enlarge their little home.

1. Aaron Green to Frank Lloyd Wright, April 20, 1939, from correspondence in the archives of the Frank Lloyd Wright Foundation (AFLWF).

2. Wright to Green, July 26, 1939, AFLWF.

3. Green to Wright, August 29, 1939, AFLWF.

4. Eugene Masselink to Green, September 2, 1939, AFLWF.

5. Masselink to Green, September 6, 1939, AFLWF.

6. Green to Masselink, September 13, 1939, AFLWF.

7. Stanley Rosenbaum to FLW, September 16, 1939, AFLWF.

8. Wright to Green, September 21, 1939, AFLWF.

9. Green to Wright, draft, September 24, 1939, AFLWF.

10. Green to Wright, final, September 24, 1939, AFLWF.

11. William Allin Storrer, *The Frank Lloyd Wright Companion* (Chicago: University of Chicago Press, 1993), 275.

12. Rosenbaum telegram to Wright, September 24, 1939, AFLWF.

13. Masselink to Green, October 25, 1939, AFLWF.

14. Building Instructions, page 2, AFLWF.

15. Green to Wright, December 1, 1939, AFLWF.

16. Wright to Rosenbaum, December 5, 1939, AFLWF.

17. Rosenbaum to Wright, December 1, 1939, AFLWF.

18. Burt Goodrich to Wright December 11, 1939, AFLWF.

19. Masselink to Goodrich, December 13, 1939, AFLWF.

20. Goodrich to Wright, December 19, 1939, AFLWF.

21. Wright to Goodrich, December 29, 1939, AFLWF.

22. Goodrich to Wright, January 4, 1940, AFLWF.

23. Wright to Goodrich, January 8, 1940, AFLWF.

24. Goodrich to Wright, January 26, 1940, AFLWF.

25. Goodrich to Wright, February 16, 1940, AFLWF.

26. Wright to Goodrich, February 20, 1940, AFLWF.

27. Reisley and Timpane, *Usonia, New York,* 63. Wright, dismissing a design by Ted Bowers, a Taliesin apprentice sent to work on the Usonia project, wrote Bowers: "Your disconnected opus—a nightmarish abuse of privilege—is at hand. Try again and don't take originality at any cost as an objective."

28. Rosenbaum to Wright, February 24, 1940, AFLWF.

29. Goodrich to Wright, February 24, 1940, AFLWF.

30. Wright to Goodrich, telegram February 28, 1940, AFLWF.

31. Wright to Goodrich, March 27, 1940, AFLWF.

32. Goodrich to Wright, March 31, 1940, AFLWF.

33. Goodrich to Wright, April 26, 1940, AFLWF.

34. Goodrich to Wright, May 12, 1940, AFLWF.

35. Wright to Goodrich, May 15, 1940, AFLWF.

36. Masselink to Goodrich, June 4, 1940, AFLWF. See also Vincent Joseph Scully, *Frank Lloyd Wright* (New York: G. Braziller, 1960). Scully describes Wright's personality as that of a true genius, a lonely, heroic visionary who is completely aggravated by his dependence on ordinary people to help him realize his vision.

37. Goodrich to Wright, June 7, 1940, AFLWF.

38. Goodrich to Wright, telegram, June 4, 1940, AFLWF.

39. Wright to Goodrich, telegram, June 4, 1940, AFLWF.

40. Goodrich to Wright, June 19, 1940, AFLWF.

41. Goodrich to Wright, July 15, 1940, AFLWF.

42. Rosenbaum to Julian ?, July 13, 1940.   AFLWF.

43. Rosenbaum to Wright, July 31, 1940, AFLWF.

44. Goodrich to Wright, August 11, 1940, AFLWF.

45. Wright to Clyde Pearson, secretary for the architectural licensure board of Alabama, November 27, 1940, AFLWF.

46. Frank Lloyd Wright Foundation, http://www.franklloydwright.org/index.cfm?section=research&action=display&id=78

47. Wright to Rosenbaum, March 18, 1941

48. Rosenbaum to Wright, March 21, 1941

49. Wright to Rosenbaum, April 1, 1941

50. No specifications for Wearcote exist in the Rosenbaum file. However, there is a section in the specifications for the Affleck House, built at about the same time, under the heading "The Usonian Type House. Part Four: Sheet Metal and Roofing." The directions stipulate that the roof consist of "one layer 30 lb Barrett (or equal) rag felt nailed to roof decking. Two layers of 15 lb Barrett (or equal) rag felt lapped and well mopped with genuine asphalt. Insulation on roof:

WEARCOTE TOPPING MIXED AS FOLLOWS:
1 part Portland Cement
4 parts sand
1/2 Bundle short plaster fibre per cu. ft. sand
1/2 Gal. emulsified asphalt per gal. Water

This mixture 1 1/2" thick is to be smoothly rolled down over paper roofing on fresh coating of hot asphalt. Care must be taken to pitch slightly to water outlets and all made smooth."

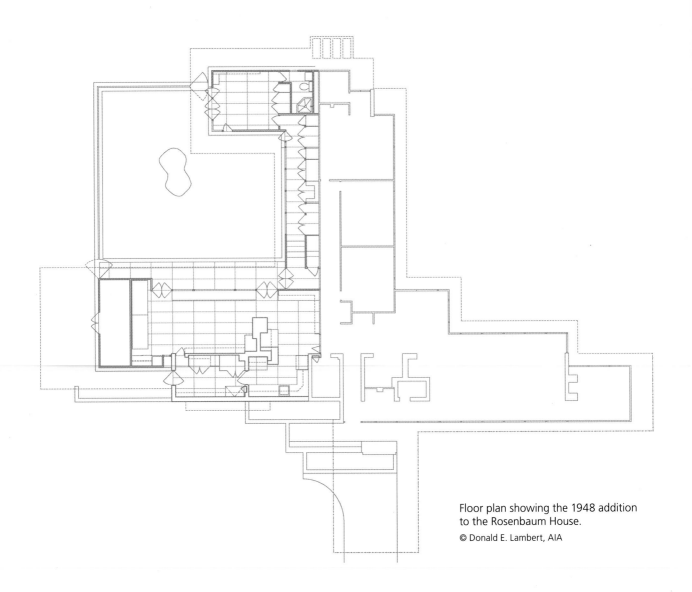

Floor plan showing the 1948 addition
to the Rosenbaum House.

© Donald E. Lambert, AIA

The 1948 Addition

With the conclusion of World War II and the end of the rationing of building materials, Americans could once again think about building homes. For the Rosenbaums, that meant an addition; they had outgrown the 1,540 square feet Wright had delivered five years earlier. They asked Wright if they might visit Taliesin West.

After their visit to Wright's desert campus, Stanley listed their needs for the addition, including a larger kitchen, a breakfast area big enough to seat six, a laundry room with a service entrance, an outside storage area for toys and tools, and a large playroom. He also called for a guest bedroom with a private bath and separate entrance. And he asked Wright to design the new wing so that it might be closed off to insure greater quiet in the original house.[1]

In February 1946, Eugene Masselink informed them that Wright would start work on the plans as soon as the group had made necessary repairs to the Arizona compound.[2] Instead, Wright's schedule dragged out until mid-September, when preliminaries were mailed. Six weeks later, Rosenbaum returned the sketches with his comments.

Stanley and Mildred Rosenbaum had learned a great deal about building from their experiences with the original house. Where there is little 1940 correspondence from Stanley to Wright about construction details, his letters now are authoritative and to the point. He now signs the letters "Stanley and Mildred Rosenbaum," instead of with just his own name.

Among his comments are detailed instructions about a utility room to house new heating equipment—apparently, he had not replaced the electric boilers, but had continued to suffer outrageous power bills. The eight-by-twelve-foot room Wright had designed seemed too small, since the Rosenbaums also wanted to keep the lawnmower and the boys' bicycles in the room. They wanted more light and ventilation in the new kitchen and dining room, as well as in the original front bathroom. Stanley wanted more bookshelves; his

The living room, with bookshelves below the windows in the front wall. However cozy in principle, the fireplaces never worked well.

Photograph © Milton Bagby

books already overflowed the existing shelves.[3]

Upon receipt of Rosenbaum's note, Wright sent him a bill for 2 percent of the anticipated cost of $15,000.[4] Rosenbaum sent the money and asked if he and Mildred might again visit Taliesin West in January.[5] Sometime between then and May 1947, the Rosenbaums decided to delay the project until the following year, but Rosenbaum wanted Wright to give him an estimate of how much cypress would be needed. He wanted to order cured cypress well ahead of schedule to insure that they did not have to use green wood when they started.[6] Stanley had approximate amounts by June,

but soon discovered that finding cypress of any sort was still a problem. Meanwhile, he still had the same questions for Wright about the size of the new utility room, the kitchen ventilation, and so forth, which he repeated in even more detail. Raising a new issue, Rosenbaum wondered if the chimneys might not be reworked. "We have never had the satisfactory use of either of our fireplaces," he complained.[7]

Wright was now eighty-one years old. He was involved in the design of the Galesburg and Parkwyn Village Usonian communities in Michigan. The return of America's military men to civilian life had created a

The playroom had four bunk beds suspended from the ceiling. Each of the four Rosenbaum boys had a small drawer and a large drawer of his own in the built-in dresser at left.

Photograph © Milton Bagby

boom in home building as well as family size. Wright was now in great demand, and one had to wait longer for answers from him than had been the case a decade earlier. Perhaps Wright was not convinced that Rosenbaum was serious, given that there had already been several delays on Rosenbaum's part. In January, Wright put it to them succinctly: "Dear Rosenbaums: Are you determined to go ahead? If so we will do our best. Will answer your questions soon."[8]

"YES WE MUST GO AHEAD," Stanley's return telegram asserted. "WE DO NOT HAVE ROOM FOR ALL OUR CHILDREN AS MATTERS STAND. WE HAVE LOCATED OUR CYPRESS."[9] By now, Stanley and Mildred had three boys with a fourth child on the way.

Wright was ready with a design for the space, but technical matters regarding the gravity heating system needed to be resolved. There followed a frantic search for the original as-built drawings, which nobody seemed to have. By the time a set was located—Burt Goodrich still had a set of prints—and decisions could be made, another month had passed. The Rosenbaums had inquired about a supervisor, suggesting that one arrive before mid-March in order to best take advantage of the building season.

Light comes from several sources in the 1948 kitchen, including skylight, clerestory, and fluorescent uplight.

Photograph © Milton Bagby

Wright turned to a former apprentice.[10] Benjamin Dombar was an architect from Cincinnati who had gone out on his own after serving in the Air Force during the war. He had trained under Wright from 1934 until 1941. Dombar was interested, but the arrangement would be different from that with Burt Goodrich. Because he had a practice up and running, as well as a wife and a young family under way, Dombar could not take up temporary residence in Florence; instead, he would make periodic visits. This met with the approval of the Rosenbaums, who were by now more comfortable with the process of construction.

The young architect met with the owners in early April and reached an agreement to proceed.[11]

It was also during this period that Mildred Rosenbaum took charge of the project, beginning with a very businesslike letter on March 30 and continuing with handwritten correspondence between her and Dombar throughout the rest of the construction.

At her suggestion, a two-foot fluorescent lighting fixture was built in beneath each of the bookshelves that line the four bunks in the boys' new bedroom, previously called the playroom. Elsewhere in the letter, she argued for more light. She attached sketches that detailed the

The 1948 addition. The family lived in the house during construction, and curtains were already up in the playroom.

Photograph courtesy The Frank Lloyd Wright Foundation, Taliesin West, Scottsdale, AZ

The 1948 addition. Wright made it a point to design the Usonians so that more space could easily be grafted onto earlier sections.

Photograph courtesy The Frank Lloyd Wright Foundation, Taliesin West, Scottsdale, AZ

A view of the carport, with the 1948 addition in the background. Supervising architect Benjamin Dombar was pleased with the way the addition seamlessly blended into the original house.

Photograph © Milton Bagby

problem of recessing additional fixtures in the ceiling.[12] In some cases, she acted as an on-site project manager, sending detailed notes to Dombar about design aspects that worked or were not working.[13]

It must not have been easy. "If I get through this summer with my sanity, it will be a miracle. With all the children underfoot in the debris, it's really something."[14]

In September, Dombar asked Wright to consider adding a carport on the end of the addition beyond the storage room. The Rosenbaums had decided to buy a second car, a station wagon for Mildred. Dombar suggested that if they moved quickly before further construction made the change difficult, a cantilevered carport roof could be added to the design and a short semicircular driveway routed from the side street.[15] Eugene Masselink sent Wright's approval and a sketch for the new overhang within a week.[16]

Dombar visited the Rosenbaum job regularly, every four to five weeks. The addition was completed by Thanksgiving, and Dombar made his final inspection in the first week of December. "One can't tell where the original house and the addition meet," he wrote to Wright. "They merge so neatly."[17] He would work again for Wright, this time closer to home, building a

Usonian house in 1954 for Cedric and Patricia Boulter in Cincinnati.[18] Dombar practiced in Ohio until his retirement and was a prominent member of the local chapter of the American Institute of Architects.

When the Rosenbaum addition was complete, Dombar sent a copy of the final costs to Wright on December 27, but his figures are lost from the records. The original estimate was $15,000, but the longstanding anecdotal final cost is somewhere between $40,000 and $50,000.

If the cost overrun troubled the Rosenbaums, it is not evident in any of Mildred's later correspondence. Perhaps, by then, they were prepared by experience for the costs to exceed estimates. They were also no longer anxious newlyweds but veterans at business and family life. There was a price one paid to have a house by Frank Lloyd Wright, something they knew going into the project. If Dombar visited the site once a month, that means that the bulk of supervision fell to Mildred. The detail and perceptiveness of her correspondence with Dombar clearly indicate that she understood the design and the process of its construction.

When the addition was finally completed, she blessed it this way: "I have finished my routine housewarmings and am starting to live the normal, happy life I've been waiting for these many years. It's wonderful."[19]

1. Rosenbaum to Wright, January 23, 1946, AFLWF.
2. Masselink to Rosenbaum, February 23, 1946, AFLWF.
3. Rosenbaum to Wright, October 30, 1946, AFLWF.
4. Wright to Rosenbaum, November 7, 1946, AFLWF .
5. Rosenbaum to Wright, November 9, 1946, AFLWF.
6. Rosenbaum to Wright, May 16, 1947, AFLWF.
7. Rosenbaum to Wright, October 16, 1947, AFLWF.
8. Wright to Rosenbaum, January 17, 1948, AFLWF.
9. Rosenbaum to Wright, telegram, January 20, 1948, AFLWF.
10. Wright to Benjamin Dombar, telegram, February 21, 1948 AFLWF.
11. Dombar to Wright, undated; mid-April, 1948, AFLWF.
12. M. Rosenbaum to Dombar, July 28, 1948.
13. M. Rosenbaum to Dombar, August 3, 1948.
14. M. Rosenbaum to Dombar, August 9, 1948.
15. Dombar to Wright, September 14, 1948, AFLWF.
16. Masselink to Rosenbaum, September 23, 1948, AFLWF.
17. Dombar to Wright, December 9, 1948, AFLWF.
18. William Allin Storrer, *The Frank Lloyd Wright Companion* (Chicago, University of Chicago Press, 1993), 407.
19. M. Rosenbaum to Dombar, April 21, 1949, AFLWF.

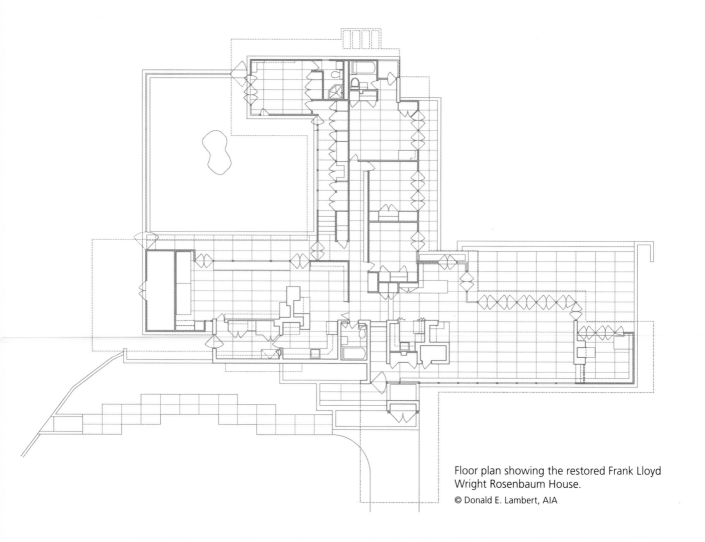

Floor plan showing the restored Frank Lloyd Wright Rosenbaum House.

© Donald E. Lambert, AIA

THE RESTORATION

Shortly after the city of Florence purchased the Rosenbaum House, museum director Barbara Broach went to take a long look at the challenge the mayor had just given her. The midday sky was dark, promising the kind of gusty, violent rain that comes with the heat of summer in the Deep South.

As she went inside, Broach remembered what her husband, Barry—himself an architect and the city planner for Florence—had told her: *If you go in the house, leave all the doors open behind you. If you hear a cracking noise, run outside.* The building had, after all, been condemned. The city inspector, convinced that it might not withstand the next real wind, said it was unsafe and wanted it torn down.

Inside, the house was musty with the smell of mildew. Outside, the rain started, quickly becoming a deluge. Water began to pour through the ceiling, at first in trickles, then in one steady cascade after another, falling to the floor or into buckets and kitchen pans knowingly left behind by Mildred Rosenbaum.

Barbara Broach began to cry.

Guest bedroom, January 2000, prior to demolition. The entire roof was covered with a plastic tarp.
Photograph © Donald E. Lambert, AIA

Mildred Rosenbaum had not lived in the house for several months. A fall during the winter had convinced her to leave the house she had come to as Stanley Rosenbaum's new bride sixty years earlier. As sale papers were being signed at the closing, Broach asked Mildred if she had any second thoughts about selling the house.

"She looked at me, put her fingertips on her shoulders, then raised them slowly and said, 'I feel like the weight of the world has been taken away.' I really needed to hear that," Broach recalls.

Looking at the condition of the house, Broach now understood what Mildred meant. The upkeep of any house, let alone a masterpiece with a leaking roof, would be a daunting task for any homeowner past eighty. The house was not only a great part of Mildred's life—perhaps part of her definition of herself—it was an important place. That was a responsibility she wanted to pass on.

The Rosenbaum House is a Florence landmark. Over the years, it had been open to the public on special occasions. For every visitor who had been inside the house, hundreds more had driven down Riverview Drive and seen its long horizontal lines of red Tennessee Valley brick and its cypress siding, varnished and aged to a reddish brown.

It is not the only landmark in Florence, however. The city is the birthplace of W. C. Handy, the African American composer widely known as "the Father of the Blues." Handy's simple log cabin is preserved as a museum containing a collection of his sheet music, instruments, and personal effects. The city also maintains Pope's Tavern, an inn and stagecoach stop that dates to the early 1800s. A few blocks from the Rosenbaum House on the bluff above the Tennessee River sits a pre-Columbian Indian mound, the largest domiciliary mound in the Tennessee Valley. A museum there details the life of ancient Native Americans who occupied the region long before the Cherokees, Chickasaws, and Creeks.

These landmarks are all city museums. Mayor Eddie Frost directed Barbara Broach to bring the Rosenbaum House into the system. Frost had been mayor for over sixteen years. A veteran politician and a man of considerable charm, he had built up years of the goodwill and personal markers that a politician needs to tackle a difficult project. "He was not a student of architecture, but he had the ability to step outside his own interests and look at a thing," Broach remembers. "If he saw the value in something, he would pursue it wholeheartedly, which he did with the Rosenbaum House."

While at a conference in Boston in early 1999, Alvin Rosenbaum, now a planner and civic activist residing in northern Virginia, approached Barry Broach with the idea that the city of Florence might purchase the house from his mother. Intrigued, Broach forwarded Alvin Rosenbaum's suggestion to Mayor Frost.

At about that same time, the city was studying a proposal to acquire another historic property, the Martin Bounds House, an antebellum mansion.

"Several of us went to the mayor and told him that the Bounds House might be a fine old place, but the Rosenbaum House was internationally known, a truly significant building," said Don Lambert, a Florence architect who consulted on the Bounds property.

Mayor Frost, hearing the same idea from two different sources, decided to pass on the Bounds House and instead entered into negotiations with the Rosenbaums. By the summer of 1999, the parties agreed to a price of $75,000—a low price for a treasure, but it was a treasure in desperate shape. The sale included any furnishings left behind. The Rosenbaums removed personal items and memorabilia, but left several pieces of the original Wright-designed furniture. Frost gave Broach the key to the house and instructed her to save what she could.

"We knew it was raining inside the house. I immediately went there with Mary Nicely, my assistant, and we started cataloguing the contents and removing them to safe storage."

Before any program of restoration could begin, the house had to be stabilized to prevent further damage. Mayor Frost asked Broach and Lambert to meet with him to recommend first steps. "Barbara and I agreed that our worst problem was the roof and that we had to start there first," Lambert recalled. Dave Marbury of Craig Construction Company was contacted by Lambert and Broach to oversee construction for the restoration, since Craig had helped Mrs. Rosenbaum with the house in recent years. Don Holden, construction superintendent for Craig, had done some patchwork repairs to the roof. Holden and his crew, which included Donnie Wilson, Charles Moore, and Holden's son Clay, spread plastic tarps across the roof to temporarily hold back the water. Inside, they draped vulnerable features with clear plastic sheeting. Water damage was visible

Bedroom ceiling. Water damage from clerestory beam extends out to eave. Plastic pipe to remove water via roof drain was an earlier, unsuccessful stopgap measure.

Study, February 2000. Termite damage was so extensive in this area that all siding was removed and much of the lower portions of the 3/4 x 12 inch pine sandwich walls replaced.

Photographs © Donald E. Lambert, AIA

everywhere. Clay Holden made a discovery that alerted them to another problem: termites.

"There were some books still on the shelves in the library," Clay Holden said. "Termites had gone up inside them. They would eat the blank part of the pages, but wouldn't eat the printed part. You would open these books and thousands of tiny letters would fall out." After Lambert had inspected what he could without additional demolition, he proposed that restoration begin by removing the roof one level at a time, starting with the smallest and lowest of the roofs.

With the contents of the house removed and triage performed on the roof, Broach and Lambert met again with Frost to set up an official plan for bringing the Rosenbaum House back to life. Alvin Rosenbaum had mentioned during the negotiations that he believed it would take a million dollars to restore the house.

"I told the mayor that I thought that figure was high, but it wouldn't be cheap," Lambert said. "Renovation is always more expensive than new construction, and we were dealing with a famous building in terrible shape, which would just add to the cost. Still, I guessed we could do it for under a million. I just couldn't tell him how far under a million."

This was not comforting news to Broach. She would be the one responsible for dealing with contractors and costs. She had worked for the city since 1976, had been involved in bringing each of the city's museums into being, and knew the pitfalls involved in working with an old historic structure.

"I had to be honest with Mayor Frost. I told him that if we took bids on the work and costs went up every time we found a hidden problem, then nobody would be happy, and I would be the unhappiest one of all. If we were to do the work on that basis, I wanted him to find someone else."

Frost was faced with a complex problem. The city had taken possession of the house, spending $75,000 of public money for the title, plus a small amount of emergency funding to stabilize the structure. Swathing the roof in plastic was a stopgap measure; the house needed immediate attention. Even after the most rigorous inspection, there was no way to know exactly how much work was required or what it would cost. Open-ended funding of any project, public or private, is rarely approved, yet this was the prospect with which Frost was faced.

Frost met with members of the city council, including Dick Jordan, who would later be appointed mayor of Florence following Frost's death, and Steve Pierce, then council president. Frost laid out a plan to restore the Rosenbaum House on a cost-plus basis, using one penny of the city's sales tax as a funding source. Pierce endorsed the plan and worked within the council to build support. Jordan, who inherited the project in his administration, would see the plan through to its conclusion.

In October 1999, with a funding system now in place, Frost met again with Broach and Lambert, instructing them to do the job right but to hold the line on costs. He told them that they were to be like a three-legged stool: Broach, Lambert, and the mayor would lean on each other for support. "Just imagine," he joked with them, "that only the whole world is looking over your shoulder."

Lambert then asked architect John Eifler to consult on the project. Eifler had been instrumental in restoring the Seth Peterson cabin at Lake Dalton, Wisconsin,[1] and had also assisted in a renovation of the first Jacobs House, a Usonian that was very similar to the Rosenbaum House. The Peterson cabin, a little one-bedroom jewel box of a house, was one of Wright's last Usonian designs. Lake Dalton had become a state park. The Peterson cabin, part of the state's acquisition, had been empty for years. While its stone walls had remained in good shape, much of the roof and ceiling had been lost to the elements. Eifler had been forced to completely rebuild the roof of the Peterson cabin. The gravity heating system also had to be replaced. The flagstone floor was pulled up and numbered, rock by rock, for reinstallation after the piping was replaced. Lambert believed he was facing the same situation with the Rosenbaum House and looked to Eifler for advice.

After an inspection visit, Eifler made a list of recommendations that included replacing the roof and restoring the gravity heat system, which had long since stopped functioning. Everyone agreed that the roof structure was compromised and needed replacement, but the matter of gravity heat put Lambert in conflict with Wright's original design for the first time.

"The issue was not only heat but air-conditioning," Lambert recalled. "Most of Wright's designs were built farther north, where summer heat isn't so oppressive. Alabama is different." With a low, flat roof and no insulation, the house heats up quickly in summer. Wright intended that a draft would be created and the house naturally cooled by opening the doors and clerestory windows.

"When it's 100 degrees outside with 100 percent humidity, that's not much help. Furthermore, we were going to make a public museum of the house. There would be a real problem with security if we were to leave all the doors and windows open in the summer. Plus, we knew the public was accustomed to air-conditioning and their experience would be negatively affected."

When Wright designed the Rosenbaum House, air-conditioning for residential structures was a rarity and had only recently come to commercial buildings. Theaters and department stores in the 1930s and 1940s hung great banners across their entrances with bold letters rendered as if snow covered, encouraging the public to "Come In, It's Cool Inside!" There was no mention of air-conditioning in the contract documents. The job correspondence does not indicate that the Rosenbaums ever had an expectation that the house was to be air-conditioned.

Over time, as systems became more available, the Rosenbaums installed air-conditioning with varying results. There were two rooftop units over the kitchen area. Condensation from the units found its way through the roof penetrations for the ducts, ruining more ceilings and woodwork. The ducts, with nowhere to hide, ran exposed along the ceiling, and not artfully. "It was hideous," Lambert recalled.

Elsewhere, the Rosenbaums had installed a through-wall unit that spanned a sandwich wall between two bedrooms, with half of the unit serving each room. A similar air conditioner was installed in the guest room in the 1948 addition. These motel-type units were used year-round for heating and cooling.

Restoring the gravity heating system posed another problem. Repair necessitated tearing up the concrete slab throughout the house and reinstalling not just new piping, but most of the slab as well. The cost would have been enormous and even more of the original house would have required demolition. Gravity heat was a heating method often championed by Wright and an original feature of the house, but it was also an invisible feature. New air-conditioning would provide heat as well as cooling. The gravity system was abandoned, but just how Lambert would install new air-conditioning in a house with no attic and no crawl space was a challenge that would have to be deferred until he could see what possibilities the structure offered him, consistent with Wright's design.

Before demolition, the first task was to photograph, measure, and prepare "as-built" drawings of the building as it stood. With this process completed, the crew could begin to remove the roof, one section at a time. "We would take the decking off the top and the ceiling off the bottom, then call the architects, who would come out and make sketches of the joists and any other details we uncovered," said Don Holden.

As the carpenters removed the roof over Stanley Rosenbaum's study at the end of the living room, they

With the old ceiling torn away, the steel I-beam that carries the living room roof and clerestory is visible. The beam is anchored in the chimneys at either end of the room.

Photograph © Donald E. Lambert, AIA

discovered that the entire section of roof was resting on two two-by-fours.

"After they built the original deck, they came back and sawed out a channel to install the lighting," Holden said. "They cut through every joist but two. It stayed up all those years because it was already tied into the rest of the roof deck. When we got it uncovered so we could take it down, it just fell in a heap."

While the crew removed roof sections, Don Lambert and Glen Smith, a journeyman CAD draftsman with Lambert's firm, delineated the plan for installing replacement joists, carefully following Wright's original joist scheme, which called for three

Reframing the roof over the new kitchen and the guest wing hallway, April 2000.

Photograph © Donald E. Lambert, AIA

toenailed two-by-fours laminated to form a larger joist. To prevent deflection, Lambert added steel flitch plates sandwiched between joists at key points. Wright's original specifications called for a roof pitch of 1/8 inch to the foot. Measurements of the top plates along the walls revealed the house to be almost perfectly level, so Lambert instructed the carpenters to shave long shims from two-by-fours that added the pitch Wright had required. The reinstalled roof is technically a hip roof, but it appears flat to the naked eye.

A treated linen roofing canvas used by Taliesin craftsmen to resurface the roof in 1969 had been painted Cherokee red, Wright's signature color. Lambert was able to find a heavy-duty thermoplastic PVC roll roofing product manufactured by Sarnafil that was available in a color very similar to Cherokee red. As the decks went back into place, the Sarnafil membrane was applied and the roof reflashed with new copper. The gravel stop, which had been added to the roof at some point to deal with the water problem, was removed, and Wright's original fascia design restored.

Lambert added another component to the original roof design: insulation. Two-inch polyurethane foam was installed between the joists and vented to the eaves, where a narrow bronze-screened venting slot, original to the house, had been cut in the soffit to exhaust the ceiling space.

Wright once referred to red tidewater cypress as "the wood of the gods." He specified it often, and it was a mainstay feature of his Usonian designs. It is light but strong, has a tight grain, weathers to a beautiful gray, and is all but impervious to insects and rot. Nowhere is this better demonstrated than at the Rosenbaum House. Despite sixty years of water problems and, as the crew would discover, pervasive termite damage, very few cypress boards had to be replaced during the restoration.

"We began to remove the outer boards, one at a time," Clay Holden recalled. "They were held on with brass screws that were very strong. We tore up some screwdriver tips, but rarely stripped the slot on those screws. We were actually able to reuse most of them. When we got inside the walls, we found that termites had damaged most of the 3/4-x-12 inch pine in the middle of the sandwich panels. They didn't touch the cypress. Most of the damage was low in the wall, rarely above two feet, but in some places that part of the inner wall was completely gone. We were able

The living room under reconstruction, January 2001.

Guest bedroom, February, 2000. New wiring is being installed. The lowest roofs were replaced first.
Photographs © Donald E. Lambert, AIA

Recessed light well in ceiling with cutout panels unique to the Rosenbaum House. Wright crafted a different fretwork design for each Usonian.

Original bakelite switch cover in bedroom, with site-built wooden base and top ornaments.

Photographs © Milton Bagby

to repair the wall with pieces of boards tied back into the original.

"It wasn't so difficult when we could reach the problem from the exterior. The interior boards, however, were interlaced, with each board and batten alternating in and out at the corners. To take a board off in the middle of the wall or down low, you had to start at the top and remove them in order. It was like a Chinese puzzle. We numbered each board or we never could have put it all back together."

As portions of the wall and ceiling were removed, the house was rewired and brought up to code. Because the walls were solid and not hollow like standard two-by-four residential framing, some wiring had to be routed into channels cut to admit flexible conduit. There are places in the house where wooden trim originally covered wiring that could not be hidden. All those details were rewired and remain in place.

The recessed light channels that run throughout the house had to be updated. With lighting still provided by incandescent bulbs behind white glass covered by distinctive fretwork panels, the rebuilt light trough is now backed with a reflective metal panel; it has horizontal sockets as opposed to the original box-mounted vertical porcelain sockets fitted to the underside of the roof deck. The fretwork cypress panels covering the lighting trough have a repeated geometric pattern cut out by jigsaw. This pattern is repeated on panels over the clerestory windows. Wright designed a unique fretwork pattern for each Usonian project; these patterns are some of the most well-known identifiers of Wright's work.

In more than one location, Clay Holden discovered that the insulation on the original wiring had completely disintegrated and bare wires ran from one junction to the next. "It's a good thing so much of that wood was wet all the time, or there would have been a fire. We were trying to temporarily run our job trailer with a drop cord from the guest bedroom. When we plugged it in, we got a little tingle, so we checked it out. We traced it back to the panel, where we found that at some point a 110-volt outlet for the air conditioner had been wired for 220 volts. It's a miracle somebody didn't get electrocuted."

Reconstruction of the original cantilevered carport roof required additional stiffening. Tied into the masonry mass at the kitchen wall and propped atop a small tool closet near the front door, the roof extended almost

Horizontal light fixture replaced standard box-mounted porcelain sockets after new rigid insulation made ceiling depth shallower.

1940 carport, showing water damage to fascia.
Photographs © Donald E. Lambert, AIA

1948 carport just before demolition. Cantilever is propped up by two-by-four trellises.

Staggered courses of roof joists show how finished carport ceiling steps back. Original I-beams were stiffened with steel channel.

Photographs © Donald E. Lambert, AIA

twenty feet from the closet wall. "It moved around like a diving board, not only up and down, but torquing side to side," Lambert said. "We braced it laterally by adding more flitch plates to the diagonal roof joists. We also installed a piece of steel channel inside the I-beams to counteract their flexibility. We did something similar with the side carport, but also tied the cantilever to the slab with new steel columns installed in the utility closet. This only occurs in the 1948 addition."

By spring of 2000, all the different levels of the roof, including the skylights over the 1948 kitchen and front bath, had been replaced. The house was now completely dry inside and protected. Very little glass had been broken. Wright's mitered plate glass, which formed outside corners in the living room and graced several sections of the clerestory, had survived the demolition of the roofs and ceilings. Windows and doors were in generally good shape, requiring little more than cleaning or, in some cases, the replacement of a hinge or piece of hardware. The original site-built screen doors were refitted with bronze screen.

By now, Don Holden had turned the job over to his son Clay, and the younger Holden had settled into the painstaking task of putting the house back together like

Mitered plate glass corner at the dining area; living room is in background.

Screen door, 1948 kitchen. Bronze screen was replaced during restoration, but the hardware and time-worn door are original.

A skylight floods the tiny bathroom at the front of the 1940 house with light, making it seem larger.

Photographs © Milton Bagby

new. One of the larger chores was restoring the wood surfaces. Craig Construction called in the painting team of Leslie and Sheila Stevenson.

Wright finished cypress in several ways, but in general preferred to leave exterior surfaces unfinished to weather to a soft gray, while applying a light shellac to interior surfaces to highlight the grain. Shortly after moving in, the Rosenbaums had stained and sealed

The bedroom hallway, January 2001. The ubiquitous power sanders are present atop the cabinets.
Photograph © Donald E. Lambert, AIA

the wood, inside and out. Over the years, the finish had aged to a deep reddish brown. The restoration of the house had required the replacement of damaged wood with new in a number of places. Staining the new to match the old presented a problem that was answered by sanding the entire house, inside and out. The Stevensons sanded for months.

"There was so much wood. It was like refinishing a ship," Clay Holden said. "There were weeks during the job where all I remember was the sound of those sanders, from the time I got to work until I went home for the day." The Stevensons burned up several sanders in the process, but the result was dramatic. Bit by bit, the house was returning to the way it might have looked to Stanley and Mildred Rosenbaum as construction neared completion in the summer of 1940.

Don Lambert began researching products with which to refinish the newly sanded wood. "The Sikkens Company has a research facility in Pontiac, Michigan. We sent them samples of the old and new cypress, as well as the fir plywood we used for the ceiling. We tried to find some samples of the old wood taken from protected areas, out of the weather and direct sunlight. Sikkens formulated two different batches of stain because the new wood absorbed differently than the old wood. The exterior finish also had UV protectant added."

Meanwhile, Clay Holden was at work on the two kitchens. The original plywood cabinets in the tiny first kitchen—or Work Space, as Wright called it—were too water-damaged to preserve. They were measured and removed, and new cabinets were built to replace them. In the larger 1948 kitchen, Wright had installed metal cabinets. The builders called on Smith Brothers, whose business includes refinishing metal furniture and bathtubs. They sanded and repainted the cabinets using an automotive paint that matched the original color and finish. A period stove and refrigerator were also refurbished and installed.

The removal and replacement of the roof gave Lambert the chance to devise a solution to the problem of heating and air-conditioning the house. Working with C&H Engineers of Florence, Lambert designed a plenum in the ceiling that ran the length of the bedroom wing. The original framing placed a beam at the base of the clerestory wall consisting of four two-by-eights. The new scheme spread them out and made two beams of two two-by-eights, with the space between insulated with hard foam and used for air handling. Outlets were

New kitchen, 1948 addition. A fireplace is sited between the newer, larger kitchen and a new dining area.
Photograph © Milton Bagby

Closet in master bedroom, showing the return air grille for the new air-conditioning system. Supply grille is at the upper left of the closet side panel. Air-conditioning the restored house was a major challenge.
Photograph © Donald E. Lambert, AIA

cut in each ceiling and covered with louvered cypress grilles stained to match the ceiling. The compressor was installed outside, behind the bedroom wing, and the blower unit was hidden inside the master bedroom closet. Inside the house, the only visible evidence of the new air-conditioning is the grille in each bedroom ceiling.

For the front of the house, Lambert mounted two rooftop package units on the kitchen roof, with ductwork penetrating the roof and ceiling into the various rooms below. Concealed behind the original brick parapet, the system is not visible from ground level.

During the restoration, Mayor Eddie Frost was diagnosed with terminal cancer. While undergoing treatment in a Birmingham hospital, the popular mayor was reelected by the people of Florence to a fifth term. "The last time I saw him, he was at the house making an inspection," Barbara Broach remembered. "Without his support and belief in the house, the project might never have happened." The mayor's successor, Dick Jordan, promised Broach and Lambert that Eddie Frost's last project would be completed.

As work progressed, the public was becoming more aware of the restoration. Curiosity reached levels not seen since 1940, when people had come from all over to see the unique little flat-topped house.

"We not only had to consider the restoration of a building of historical significance, we also had to plan for the day when the public could visit. There were things we could do and things we could not do," Lambert said. The house as a museum could be made handicapped-accessible only up to a point. The bedroom doors are only twenty inches wide. Wright's floor plan changes levels several times. There is little possibility of accommodating changes without seriously altering the architecture, especially in the narrow hallways.

Routing visitors into the house via Riverview Drive posed significant safety problems. In addition, on-street parking was limited and raised the issue of congestion for the quiet neighborhood street. Lambert solved these problems with a new parking lot built on school property across a less-busy side street to the east of the house. Approaching the property from that side, visitors are routed past the 1948 addition to the original front door via a new walkway. Lambert's design, a zig-zag course of Cherokee red concrete laid out in the same two-by-four grid as the house and flanked by low

The original carport cantiliever, at almost twenty feet, had developed an unnerving flexibility prior to the restoration. Foreground shows the new two-by-four-grid walkway designed to bring visitors to the front door.

Photograph © Milton Bagby

plantings, is all but invisible from Riverview Drive and does not visually conflict with the long horizontal lines of the house.

"We wanted people to enter through the front door and see everything from the 1940 house to the 1948 addition in chronological order," Broach said.

One thing museum visitors would not see, even on the coldest of days, was a fire crackling in one of the home's fireplaces. Stanley Rosenbaum complained about them during the first winter in the house. "The main thing that bothers me is that both fireplaces smoke a great deal," he wrote to Aaron Green and Burt Goodrich, who had just arrived in Spring Green. "If you could design us some wind screens for our chimneys, which Stanfield [a local sheet metal contractor] could fix up, we would appreciate it very much."[2] Wind screens would probably not have helped. Don Holden explains: "The fireplaces were built without a smoke shelf

Rebuilding the lanai wall. Middle boards of the sandwich wall are now held in place by steel channels.
Photograph © Donald E. Lambert, AIA

or a damper. They were just a straight chimney and it's hard to make a straight chimney draw properly." The chimneys also had no masonry weathercap, so rain poured down into the fireplaces during storms. Without a damper, the chimneys couldn't be closed off to help prevent the loss of heat. The decision was made to permanently cap the chimneys.

Restoration of the Rosenbaum House began with emergency repairs in December 1999 and concluded in July 2002 with landscaping and the rebuilding of the lanai garden between the playroom and the guest bedroom. The garden work was done by Shoals Master Gardeners under the direction of Marg Webb. The garden wall around the lanai, a solid structure which repeated the reverse board-and-batten design of the house's siding, had rotted; it was replaced. Lambert capped the new wall with copper to protect it.

Working with Rebecca Meeks, the interior designer with Lambert's firm, Todd Gillreath cleaned and restored the Wright-designed furniture, which was generally in good condition. Where needed, he replaced furniture fabric to match the originals. While all rotted or termite-damaged wood was replaced throughout the house, sound portions of the walls and furniture that simply showed the effects of a lifetime of normal use were left as found.

In the end, the cost of the work approached $540,000, with another $100,000 for parking and $40,000 for landscaping. Despite the demands of saving a historic house in serious trouble, Lambert and Broach kept costs well below Alvin Rosenbaum's guess of $1 million. It was not easy. The roof and ceilings were replaced. The heating and air-conditioning system was reengineered. The carpentry and wood refinishing had more in common with yacht building than with residential construction.

Word had filtered out that the Rosenbaum House was being restored and, just as with the original construction, visitors arrived on a regular basis. "I met people from France, Germany, Kenya, South Africa, Japan," Clay Holden recalls. "Most were from the United States. People asked for souvenirs. One man asked for a piece of rotted carpet we had thrown in the dumpster. Later, he sent us a letter saying that he had framed a piece of it and had it hanging on his office wall."

Holden admits that he knew little about Frank Lloyd Wright when he started the project. By the end of the job, Holden had made a study of Wright, and visited several other Wright buildings; he felt honored to have been part of a long tradition of hands-on Wright craftsmen who had been involved in something special.

For Barbara Broach and her assistant, Mary Nicely, the process of bringing a new museum into the Florence system was complete. The process which paired Broach with Don Lambert had been long, hard work, but the two went at it in the spirit of partnership. "Don and I never had a single disagreement," Broach said. Lambert echoed her assessment: "We always worked everything out."

1. John Eifler and Kristin Visser, *Frank Lloyd Wright's Seth Peterson Cottage: Rescuing a Lost Masterwork* (Madison, Wisconsin: Prairie Oak Press, 1999). Eifler's restoration of the Peterson cabin is similar in many ways to that of the Rosenbaum House, although the work there was funded by a nonprofit conservancy and accomplished in large part by volunteers. The Peterson cabin is in a state park and can be rented, one of the few Wright homes open to the public for overnight guests.

2. Rosenbaum to Green and Goodrich, October 15, 1940, AFLWF.

AFTERWORD

James Dennis, owner of the first true Usonian, the 1936 Jacobs House, went through the process of restoring it from a state of disrepair not as severe as that of the Rosenbaum House, but not far from it.

The roof leaked everywhere, the cypress walls had been covered with asphalt paint, and a succession of residents after Jacobs had altered or simply abused the structure.

Dr. Dennis, a retired university professor, cherishes the house and is proud of the restoration, but speculates that Wright, who was forever tinkering with his own designs, might not have been so charitable. "He probably would have let it go, let it become a ruin and return to the earth," Dennis told an interviewer.[1]

The Rosenbaum House will not become a ruin. Wright's sleek design will survive into a new generation because the people of Florence, Alabama, saved it. They saved it not because they needed another museum or a tourist attraction or because, as a civic project, it satisfied some cost-to-benefit analysis. They saved it, at no small expense and human effort, because it is a work of art.

1 *Milwaukee Journal Sentinel,* May 31, 2003. James Dennis, interviewed by Whitney Gold. Architect John Eifler, who restored the Peterson cabin and consulted on the Rosenbaum project, helped Dennis restore the Jacobs House.

PHOTO GALLERY

Wright's open floor plan leads the eye from the living room into the dining area.

The rear of the house. Long lines and a low profile make the house seem more imposing than its actual size.

Photograph by Patrick Hood; © City of Florence Museums

Japanese garden in the lanai.

Photograph by Patrick Hood; © City of Florence Museums

The horizontal lines of the cypress board-and-batten courses carry through to the walls in the lanai fence.

Photograph © Milton Bagby

Exposed rafters terminate the bedroom wing.
Photograph © Milton Bagby

Lines and angles are repeated in the
roof at the rear of the guest bedroom.
Photograph © Milton Bagby

Study (left) and living room exterior demonstrate Wright's use of glass and varied ceiling heights.

Photograph © Milton Bagby

Bedroom doors open to the outside for natural living. Screen doors were added after insects and other animals made their way inside.

Photographs © Milton Bagby

The rear of the house.
Photograph © Milton Bagby

Built-in pine and plywood furniture suited Wright, who stressed simplification. The chair is an Eames, not a Wright design.
Photograph by Patrick Hood; © City of Florence Museums

Stanley Rosenbaum's study.

Photograph by Patrick Hood; © City of Florence Museums

Bedroom corridor, with bookshelf and storage cabinets. Polished woods and close quarters make this space seem more like a passageway on a yacht than the hallway of a house.

Photograph by Patrick Hood; © City of Florence Museums

Master bedroom.

Photograph by Patrick Hood; © City of Florence Museums

Stanley Rosenbaum liked his books; Wright supplied plenty of shelves for them.

Photograph by Patrick Hood; © City of Florence Museums

Serene daylight floods the hallway.

Photograph by Patrick Hood; © City of Florence Museums

Built-in bookshelves and overhead light invite
the visitor to a cozy corner.

Photograph by Patrick Hood; © City of Florence Museums

Full-height windows and glass doors open the rear
of the house to sunlight and nature.

Photograph by Patrick Hood; © City of Florence Museums

Close to the kitchen, the dining area seats six people
in a compact space.

Photograph by Patrick Hood; © City of Florence Museums

Abundant glass makes the dining area feel nearly alfresco.
Photograph by Patrick Hood; © City of Florence Museums

ABOUT THE AUTHORS

Donald E. Lambert, AIA, is a principal in the architectural firm Lambert Ezell Durham of Florence, Alabama. Barbara Kimberlin Broach directs the Kennedy Douglass Center for the Arts in Florence and is manager of that city's museum system, which includes the Rosenbaum House. Broach and Lambert directed the restoration of the Rosenbaum House. Freelance writer Milton Bagby works as an architectural draftsman for a major residential development and construction firm in Nashville, Tennessee.

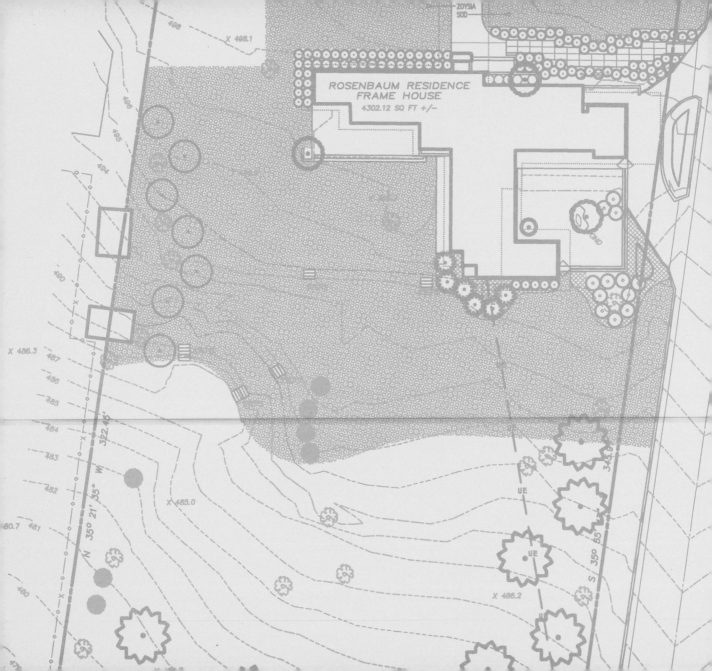

ROSENBAUM RESIDENCE
FRAME HOUSE
4302.12 SQ FT +/-